Think Like The Fish

Experiential Branding--How to Turn
Customer Fantasy into an Experience
Worthy of Extreme Loyalty and a
Five Star Online Reputation!

D. Wendal Attig

ISBN-13:
978-1507767009
ISBN-10
1507767005

First Printing, 2015

Printed in the United States of America

Income Disclaimer

This document contains business strategies, marketing methods and other business advice that, regardless of my own results and experience, may not produce the same results (or any results) for you. I make absolutely no guarantee, expressed or implied that by following the advice below you will make any money or improve current profits, as there are several factors and variables that come into play regarding any given business.

Primarily, results will depend on the nature of the product or business model, the conditions of the marketplace, the experience of the individual, and situations and elements that are beyond your control.

As with any business endeavor, you assume all risk related to investment and money based on your own discretion and at your own potential expense.

Liability Disclaimer

By reading this document, you assume all risks associated with using the advice given, with a full understanding that you, solely, are responsible for anything that may occur as a result of putting this information into action in any way, and regardless of your interpretation of the advice.

You further agree that our company cannot be held responsible in any way for the success or failure of your business as a result of the information presented below. It is your responsibility to conduct your own due diligence regarding the safe and successful operation of your business if you intend to apply any of our information in any way to your business operations.

Terms of Use

You are given a non-transferable, "personal use" license to this product. You cannot distribute it or share it with other individuals.

Table of Contents

DEDICATION

To

Janice

ACKNOWLEGEMENTS

As with my previous book, this one is the net effect of people in my life who have planted thoughts, forced me to push the envelope, and inspired me to see even my own experiences and expertise from different perspectives. Bob Kimsey, Ted Morton, Craig Johnson and "Jimbo" Hendershott at Sizzling Platter planted this concept by simply requesting the context. Without their request the metaphor would have remained undiscovered.

I would like to thank the fly fishing/meeting destinations that have chosen to promote the executive sessions I conduct for groups at their locations and who make it possible or the metaphor to come alive.

Brent Eilts who taught me the finer points of fly casting in my early experiences, and the gator in the lake we fished in Indian Rocks, Florida, who reminded me there is always a predator lurking.

Others with a stamp of influence include my late father and early fishing buddy and my Uncle Lyle, my colleagues my long term professional speaking client and colleague, Tom Shay, and my friend and spiritual influence, Charles Castle.

Special Thanks goes to Lefty Kreh, whose many books and videos were among those I studied to discover the behavior of fish and how to find them using the business end of a fly rod!

PREFACE

"Welcome to Camp SPLAT" the sign read. Here I was, deep in the Wasatch National Forest with 40 guys and gals who manage restaurants for Bob Kimsey's Sizzling Platter Corporation. We were on an executive planning retreat, but this wasn't just any retreat---not just another golf retreat at an expensive resort—this group was here to go fly fishing, to compare best practices between members of the group, and learn to competitively, "Think like the Fish". That last part was my assignment.

Camp SPLAT , an acronym for Sizzling Platter, was a combination of roughing it and eating well. When you're in the restaurant AND catering business and you choose to campout, you bring a few extras along—certainly a few steaks and the means to prepare them to perfection!

When Jim Hendershott and his crew from the training department arrived, early the previous Saturday, this campsite—located about a mile from Flaming Gorge on the world famous Green River in northern Utah-- featured nothing more than two outhouses and a fire containment pit.

By the time I arrived late afternoon on Tuesday, the campsite was outfitted with two catering trailers, a supply truck, mess tent, and a meeting tent complete with a generator, sound system, flood-lights, a stage, PowerPoint projector , banquet tables and folding chairs. This group was self sufficient—and would be for the next couple of days. Interestingly they all brought their own sleeping gear which ranged from pup tents and sleeping bags to a motor coach one manager had borrowed from his mother!

As a venue for a business meeting this one forced people to work naturally as a team, got them away from anywhere they might encounter a need to impress and presented just enough challenge to provide camaraderie, a fresh learning experience both in the sessions and with fly fishing, and resulted in a bonus--a new sense of direction. My job as I mentioned was to teach them to "Think like the fish".

VP Ted Morton insisted that marketing director, Craig Johnson ask me if I would speak for the group. Then he mentioned off-handedly that they were "going fishing." That's really where this story begins. What I'm about to share with you grew out of a simple follow-up inquiry: could I take my expertise in branding, and somehow package it in the context of this venue?

After promising I would, I began to do the research on fly fishing. While I had limited personal experience with fly fishing at the time, I quickly began to see the parallels between fly fishing and fishing for clients, customers or guests. The behavior of fish and that of customers is ironically parallel. During the more than 100 hours or research to prepare for this session, I became totally intrigued with the metaphor. As a result, an entire arm of my private practice is now devoted to sessions on brand leadership for executives on fly fishing retreats. We not only experience great fly fishing under the instruction of top guides, but we learn how to competitively, "Think like the fish, check our fly, and match the hatch" –you'll see what I mean as this book unfolds.

This book is designed to put you and your team in the competitive water, to help you discover the value of the brand experience, its impact and effect on your online reputation and brand advantage.

The metaphor AND the strategies in this book are working for other companies and they will work for yours. In the short-term, have fun with the parallels and thanks for choosing to join me on this trip. Now, let's go fishing!"

1

Standing in the River Waving a Stick

What does Fly Fishing have to do with
Experiential Branding?

At first fly fishing and branding may seem to have
nothing in common, but both are a study in
behavior—a thinking game. You might be able to
pick up the basics of either during a half-day
seminar, but continued success requires exercising
a dynamic and complex set of skills, knowledge,
analysis, observation and yes, creativity. In both
cases, you'll have to know as much about the fish
in the stream (your consumers) as you believe you
know about how to catch them.

Consumers in the marketplace and fish in the
stream are ironically similar in their behaviors.
Anglers have come to appreciate that fish are
predators of sorts and are extremely self
protective. They congregate in places along the
stream that offer protection from other predators –
places that require less energy to maintain their
positions. Both fish and consumers have a certain
attitude of entitlement.

At least in the case of trout, they orient themselves into the current so they can easily observe the food that continually floats past them. They consider each morsel based upon how much energy might be required to retrieve it. In fact, a fish will not go after ANYTHING it perceives will require more energy to consume than it may provide in return!

Consumers like the fish, are in search of products, programs and services that are packaged just right. Often their preferences are based more upon the branded experience than the quality of the product. They are looking for solutions that will predictably require little energy to consume yet offer a payback they perceive will far exceed the pay*out*!

On different days at the river, the fish find it easier to feed at varying levels in the stream. Consumers too continually adjust their consumption behavior based upon the temperature of the economy, the seasons of the year, and the offerings that drift into their limited purview.

In either case, as one of my early mentors Mike Brennan observed, "our challenge is to manage the path of least resistance," between perception and satisfaction. Whether competing in the marketplace or fly fishing at streamside, if we learn to think like the fish, our payoff will strike!

One of the many fine books John Gierach has written on fly fishing is titled, STANDING IN A RIVER WAVING A STICK. While John shares some wonderful stories about fishing for trout in the Rocky Mountains from Colorado to British Columbia, the title of the book offers another sad but comical analogy--especially when we consider the challenges of offering truly uniquely branded experiences to consumers in today's marketplace.

It may be true that some organizations are carefully orchestrating the customer's experience to extract greater brand loyalty and maximum life value of the customer, but others are simply *standing in the river waving a stick* -- -- you get the picture. We read about them in the newspaper almost daily. Fortunately just upstream as we'll see, are some better techniques and proven examples we can use for inspiration.

During early fly fishing instruction, new anglers are cautioned against fishing from a single spot on the stream for an entire day. They are encouraged instead to move carefully as they discover the behavioral patterns of the fish, read the stream and match the hatch.

Orchestrating the brand experience is very similar. It requires calculated positioning, careful consideration, applied experience, intuitive observation and often results in creative initiative outside the normal currents in your industry.

While this book can't teach you all of those skills, hopefully it will help you recognize their importance and challenge your leadership team to think like the fish as you compare the experiential branding initiatives of yours and other companies -- perhaps even those of your competitors.

Maybe you'll be motivated to wade even further into the river and implement a uniquely branded encounter--to create an exceptional customer experience, regardless of what may be accepted as the norm inside your industry.

The fly fishing analogy and the examples we'll see are meant to encourage you to step out of your comfort zone and into the stream, to look below the surface of the market (the water) then check your fly--re-examine your organization's response to the needs, wants, perceptions and desires of your customers.

With any luck, the concepts we'll discover will help you *catch* a fresh perspective that inspires you and your leadership team, then *releases* you to become more profitable. If so, I will have succeeded.

Along the way, I hope this read will be the most entertaining experience any business book has delivered lately—that you'll experience success (catch the limit) and realize more of the life value your consumers represent. Let's start our journey on the banks of the Arkansas River to see if you're ready to benefit by looking at the parallels between the behavior of fish and consumers.

2

Check Your Fly!

Streamside at Dawn—Perspectives and
Commitments

To some, it would have been simply another early
fall morning in the Rockies---just another
picturesque sunrise. But what I experienced just a
few steps behind the rustic porch rails of my
quaint log cabin deck on the banks of the
Arkansas River in Colorado's famous Sangre
deCristo mountains was nothing short of a
revelation:

Two, maybe three powerful rays of golden
sunlight burst across the crest of the crags on the
opposite side of the stream, signaling the dawn of
a new day. It wasn't just any dawn, but rather an
announcement, that in-turn within a few minutes
triggered unusual activity in the stream—an
excitement that motivated the fish into action.

These streams of almost liquid light brought
warmth to a portion of the river that is typically
shadowed at dawn. For the fish, the experience in
the stream changed as the rays of the sun
illuminated the surface of the water and generated

warmth. Suddenly, this became –for the moment—the preferred place to swim.

Why this change, this excitement, this preference? What if we examine what actually happens below the surface of the stream? Could this river experience allow us to see customers, clients and prospects from a fresh, new perspective? What if that would help us manage our customers' experience and help us produce a competitive edge? What if all we had to do was learn to "Think Like The Fish?"

At this point, we still have options.

1) Just stay here on the banks of the river, kick a few pebbles and enjoy the scenery, or

2) Go back to the cabin, climb into the waders, throw on the vest, pick up the favorite fly rod and reel and get into the flow. It's clearly time to check your fly!

As we stand here on the banks, considering those options, let me --as your guide-- make a promise to you: If you're willing to get out of the office, put on the gear and get into the stream what you'll discover through the pages of this book is how to advantage the parallels between the behavior of fish in the stream, and the behavior of consumers in the marketplace. This book offers you an opportunity to see below the surface—like wearing a pair of polarizing sunglasses—to better understand how to manage your customer's brand experience and reexamine the critical *above-the-surface* activity that affects your company's competitive edge. The objective is simple: *learn how to catch more fish than your competitors, steal customers from other offerings and increase your catch—better bottom line profits for your business and a chance to win online, where reputation is king.*

Are you in? If so, let's go back to the cabin before any more of these fish hide in the stream. Let's *gear up* to "Think Like the Fish."

3

Expectations are Key

Notes on An Early Fly Fishing Experience

Over the breakfast table one late spring morning in my senior year of high school, dad apparently sensed my enthusiasm for school was altogether missing in action, and asked about my lackadaisical attitude. I fully expected him to continue from that point, pontificating about how important these last few days of class would be, how my senior year was almost behind me and how I should simply buck up and head for the school bus.

He didn't. Instead he asked what I would rather be doing.

Since my father had previously gone on record honoring tenacity and perseverance when it came to the education of his children, this was far from his typical response. And I was not prepared with an appropriate answer. As I "hemmed and hawed," trying to think of some legitimate alternative, he suggested one. "Would you like to go fishing?" he asked without missing a beat. While I typically wasn't that excited about fishing, on this particular day any alternative would have been just fine -- -- anything but another day in the classroom!

He suggested mom pack us a lunch, and we took off toward Murphysboro, a small town in Southern Illinois with a population of 6000. It was also where one of my favorite uncles owned and operated Lyle's Sport Center. The plan was to pick up the latest in fly fishing odds and ends, get Uncle Lyle's best advice on where to go then spend the rest of the day fishing.

For more than 25 years Lyle's Sport Center had been the virtual hub of all sporting activities in Southern Illinois. The quaint little shop was chock-full of everything for the outdoor sportsmen from hunting and fishing to archery, football, baseball, soccer and more. Information from hunters and fishermen flowed freely in the little shop. Everything from fish heads to trophy racks were mounted anyplace an open spot could be created between the densely stacked and displayed merchandise that seemingly crowded every nook and cranny in the store. A trip to Lyle's Sports Center was a real experience -- -- a perfect beginning or ending to any hunting or fishing trip.

Uncle Lyle carefully chose a few fishing flies for us that day and if I remember right sent us off with a new fly rod and reel for dad, too. He recommended an ideal fishing spot in southern Missouri where the water was crystal clear -- -- naturally spring fed.

Armed with the best gear and the best advice, we crossed the mighty Mississippi River and headed for the foothills of the Ozarks. It was early afternoon.

This was the first time I had ever fished for trout. As promised, the stream was tap water clear and the trout were everywhere! In fact, there were so many fish that I often found myself stripping the line quickly, just to avoid a strike from one I thought might be too small. In retrospect, that was a great problem to have! (and one we seldom enjoy in business.)

Since this was a weekday, dad and I were the only anglers on the stream. To hungry trout, we seemed like the only option. They were ready for action. For them, it was like a one-day sale at Macy's.

What a fight ensued when the trout finally struck the fly. I will never forget that day and my first experience with fishing for trout.

More importantly, what I learned that day has translated over and over again as my career in branding, marketing and advertising has unfolded; if you have the only offering in the marketplace (stream) you'll get all the traffic --typically without a fight. Otherwise it's always going to be a battle for attention, perception, and consumer opportunity.

Orchestrating that scenario to effectively turn customer fantasy into reality is the challenge. The payoff is a sort of "catch and release" program that extends the life value of the customer and reduces the hard costs of customer acquisition and retention. That savings floats directly to your bottom line profitability.

Ensuring the customer's experience to the point where they prefer your offering over all the other options in the stream is why learning to "think like the fish," is imperative to your brand and your company's future.

4

A Better Offer than the "Naturals"

Big Cedar Lodge— Masters at Moving the
Mindset

Successful branding initially involves creating the
perception you want to own in the Marketplace of
the Mind. Just as you want the fish in the stream to
believe your offer is preferable to the "naturals,"
you have an opportunity with your consumers to
create the perception that you indeed offer extreme
value. Done right, this initial positioning will
create an opportunity to deliver your form of
reality—show your stuff—do what you do best.
Assuming both the positioning and the delivery
exceed expectations, you'll catch the fish! And
they in-turn with online feedback and reviews will
help you catch even more. Let's look below the
surface and see how it works.

Driving south on US-Highway 65 out of Branson,
Missouri through the world renowned Ozark
Mountains, it isn't long before the signs point out
an option to turn right on to county road 86. Take it
and you'll be going west toward Table Rock Lake
and if you're lucky, a stay at Big Cedar Lodge for

fishing, hunting, boating and other outdoor sports. Developed and operated by the Bass Pro Shops, this property is a premier location for conferences and family fun.

Not long after you make that right hand turn onto county road 86 –what Midwesterners would still consider "the hard road," meaning anything other than dirt or gravel—you begin to see the billboard signs for Big Cedar Lodge.

At first they look like a throwback to the 50's and 60's—those flashy tourist-trap style billboards along great highways like Route 66, meant to lure the tourist in to sit a spell and spend some money. (So far they are working just like they did on my father and maybe yours more than 50 years ago!)

As I recall they start when you're not too far from the main entrance to Big Cedar Lodge and are placed at strategic locations to inform you of just how close you are getting, and to build excitement.

In the back seat, the kids are crazy with anticipation which translates into hyperactivity. In the front, you and your spouse are both on cell phones, wrapping up a few issues at the office. Thoughts about how inappropriate the timing on this trip might be are clouding your own anticipation.

The final countdown is progressively noted by still more billboards announcing Big Cedar Lodge will be

1500 feet ahead, then 1000 feet ahead, then 500 feet ahead and finally that you have arrived!

The words: Big Cedar Lodge arch across the entrance to the property, suspended between twin towering, rough-hewn, pine poles welcoming you and visually framing the promises the billboards claimed.

As you follow the huge arrow on the sign directing you to turn right and go between the legs of the welcome entrance, you flashback to summer camp and family vacations by car and roughing it somewhere--perhaps in a state or national park. But it's only a flashback.

You're still dealing mentally with Fred and Emily and this week's sales activity report and wondering whether Stephanie was copied by email and if the report actually got pushed through to Robert for review on the beach in Honolulu……

You don't know it, but you're about to experience another type of distraction. This time it will be magic. And it will be intentional.

Just 500 yards or so inside the main entrance is when you realize that this road you're on is awfully narrow. In fact, it is only one lane! And the trees come right up to the edge of the road. Just then the road starts down a rather steep incline and you wonder what to do if you meet another car coming toward you. No place to pass! What if this was icy?

At the bottom of the hill, you make a hairpin curve to the left, still pondering the narrowness of the road, when you see it; a couple of forked sticks with a metal-style fishing stringer suspended between them. Hanging from the stringer is the shadowy, side-by-side, silhouetted cutout of several fish. Stenciled across the cutout are the words, "Ya shoulda been here yesterday!" Your immediate response is, "Why?" followed by increasing curiosity—the desired effect.

Almost before you have a chance to explore your curiosity, the top of the hill emerges and reveals yet another set of forked sticks, stringer and silhouette. This one completes the earlier thought…, "The Biguns were Bitin', " it says.

Now you pick up the pace, both physically and mentally. The thought of having missed the big ones is unacceptable—even if you didn't come here to fish! But you rationalize that maybe if you hurry, there's still time!

A couple more bends in the road finds you once again on a downhill slope—this time you realize there is s a stream crossing the road. No way can you retreat. No possibility you can maneuver a u-turn in this massive SUV (The one you claim your spouse insisted you buy.) You'll have to ford the stream. Really? Yes, really.

About this time, you notice the waterfall to your right. The kids could almost touch it with the window rolled down. "Good, the water looks like its only about 6 inches deep across the road!" you note.

As you silently admonish yourself for the 4x4 virtues you personally insisted the family would need at such a time like this, you look up. There, unfolding before you is the incredible Big Cedar Lodge complex with all of its rustic charm! The setting is breathtaking. You   are   in   the moment.

You've arrived and you're happy to be here. The Bass Pro Shops have managed to transport you mentally from the cares of life to the leisure you're about to experience in less than 300 seconds!

Later you'll discover that the architecture, the décor and the details are all carefully designed and implemented to reinforce the brand experience that innocently started for you and your family, way out on county road 86. (You'll also discover later that the exit from the complex is a hi-speed four-lane one-way getaway.) This entry experience was intentional, and it worked.

As a guest at Big Cedar Lodge, activities are all consistent with outdoor sports. It isn't a put-off that a trophy deer head is mounted on the wall in your lodge room. It's equally unique that a chuck wagon catering and entertainment troupe will meet your corporate or association group on one of the Table rock Lake islands only accessible by boat for a campfire evening of customized fun, tailored to your specific needs.

The Big Cedar Lodge leadership team has read the stream, studied the behavior of the fish they hope to catch, and matched the hatch with options and accoutrements that make sense.

From trout flying through the bases of nightstand lamps to antler chandeliers to log slab coffee tables and custom Big Cedar andirons facing the fireplaces, everything is meant to enhance this experience, reinforce your choice and you're your referrals.

The overall experience is consistent throughout and congruent with the location. In the context of the other options you could have chosen, this package and this presentation are superior to any other offer in the stream. They have produced a unique, branded experience that is synonymous with Big Cedar Lodge—an experience you will forever associate as a new standard of excellence--and one you will not soon forget. You have experienced "Catch and Release" in its finest form. You will be back for more.

Quick Question: Is your business offering an experience that is better than the "naturals"—what the other guys do—what is generally expected in your category? Are you delivering an experience that deserves superior feedback and warrants 5-star ratings?

Our company works with those who want to develop and maintain a five star rating online. What they have discovered is that people are not only willing to initially include them in their consideration, but are willing to pay more for their services if they have higher ratings and superior reviews!

When a customer/patient/resident is willing to provide positive feedback and 5-star ratings, they have become a loyal customer.

Because of the rapid switch to online research by prospects to consider what company they will choose, active customer feedback not only solidifies their loyalty but becomes the catalyst for sending more pre-qualified and pre-sold new business to the company of choice—prospects that may never be reached otherwise –prospects no TV or radio or newspaper or magazine or other traditional advertising could ever reach.

The brand experience you craft and deliver can start a chain reaction that has the power to either destroy or build your business.

5

Attractors

Coffee-2-Go -- Selling the *Smell* of Success

Imagine this: a drive through coffee experience that begins which a dash right off the main arterial you take to work. As you lower the window to order, you immediately smell the coffee—fine Illy Italian coffee and you can't help but smell the aroma of fresh, baked on site Danish pastry. Your branded experience has begun. Your order is cheerfully confirmed by the barista whom you discover is outfitted accordingly at the pick-up window.

If you failed to order fine pastry with your coffee, you are shown a small selection to further entice your appctitc.

While your payment is processed, you are handed a complimentary copy of the local morning paper with a sticker attached inviting you to park and use the Wi-Fi if you would rather connect while you enjoy your pastry and coffee.

As your order is confirmed and presented, you hear the words, "See you tomorrow!" The exit merges you right back into traffic and you're back in the mainstream of your life. More importantly, you fully intend to see them again tomorrow! You may choose to park and enjoy the experience on the inside when you have more time another day.

Not all great experiential marketing or branding initiatives succeed. Even with the best of intentions, a clear focus on the objectives and a hip pocket full of great ideas, business start-ups sometimes fail. Often in hindsight, the founders were lacking a key ingredient. They may have started fishing without resources to wade further into the stream as we'll see in this classic example.

Start-ups are often a test-bed for great experiential concepts. Many of these ventures begin because the founders have assembled a host of differentiators that have the potential to deliver a brand experience clearly superior to existing competition. Entrepreneurs often proceed at this point, not because they should, but because they can—the excitement supercharges their efforts and many time supersedes their judgment—and often a voice of reason along the trail never surfaces to pose the critical questions. Because "they can", many do without the assistance of a guide.

Sadly in today's business climate, too many of these ventures are simply under-funded. While the business model and certainly the brand experience have significant merit, they simply choke before the right connection can be made with investors who understand the potential and are willing to get into the current and take the bait. Along the way, limited capital often forces these groups to make less than ideal location or packaging choices that may stretch the resources, but compromises success.

The operational and promotional capital simply isn't strong enough to sustain the business from infancy to survival in a crowded stream. Much like choosing the right fly, Failure doesn't make these offerings any less compelling or the brand experience any less intriguing but rather proves that the fish their targeting in the investment stream may be feeding at a different level as we'll see in this example.

Coffee-2-Go was a start-up in the Tampa Bay market in early 2005. The founders were experienced in the fast-food sector, so the drive through experience was one they understood as both the anglers and the fish. Fundamentally they believed that the drive-thru-coffee customer was underserved.

The concept was relatively straight forward.

- Locate on a high-traffic arterial with easy entrance and egress.

- Expand the menu to include food items most drive-thru-coffee options didn't offer

- Package it all with an experiential presentation that was more attractive than other offerings in the stream.

Was the brand worth the premium? Was the experience worth the effort? Was it superior to the competition—the norm? How would you answer those questions in this case, and about your own offerings?

6

Never Spook the Fish!

Dimmitt Cadillac—Managing the Moments of
Truth That Turn Customer Fantasy into Reality

Since most fly fishing is done in the stream, where
the angler finds plenty of room to accommodate
the back and forward casts, this positioning
requires wading into the water with a certain
modicum of care and concern. Much like wading
into your market with calculated finesse, the big
idea is to avoid "spooking" the fish, be consistent
and position your offer with differentiating
attraction.

Most of us can relate to a trip to the local car
dealership. Whether for service or for the purchase
of a new car, this experience has notoriously
become one of the least favorite activities for the
majority of Americans. Why? Because there is a
fear of the unknown.

Just as the fish are wary of the added movement in
the water, the shadows cast by the angler, and at

times are spooked by the presentation of the fly--if not presented properly--so consumers are cautious when approached by sales or service professionals at the dealership, and wary of the overall experience. Sadly, more often than not, the experience warrants the fear. The idea of being "taken" or experiencing the typical hassle-factor simply isn't acceptable.

But it doesn't have to be that way.

In fact it *isn't* like that at all in one of America's top luxury car dealerships in Clearwater, Florida.

Dimmitt Cadillac –voted #1 Cadillac Dealership for Customer Service in the U.S.--like many dealerships is a reputable firm with a lengthy track record, but that's where the similarity stops.

Dimmitt's nationally recognized approach to capitalizing on the life value of a customer really started when they began to examine the profit centers in the dealership. They determined that profitability could be extended if they simply redesigned the service experience for their customers. In the process they have created an extremely loyal customer base.

Michael F. Brennan Jr., an early mentor of mine that I often quote, once said, "It's all about managing the path of least resistance between the offer and the consumer's wallet."

In our fly fishing analogy, it's all about matching the hatch—choosing a fly pattern that matches what the fish are feeding on—then delivering in a fashion that does not spook the fish and makes the offer more attractive than the *naturals*. This case demonstrates the point.

When you arrive on the red carpet drive- through service area at Dimmitt, you are met by the customary service representative (the same one is permanently assigned to you to help build on-going connection between you and the dealership), you share the concerns you have, and then are handed off personally to the concierge. This is an FTE who after a couple of visits knows you by name. The concierge briefs you on several time-killing options you may have during your stay-- based upon your personal interests—and also reminds you of the services they offer.

Your options include use of the putting green with an invitation to take part in a daily competition. This is a professionally manicured green on the front lawn of the dealership, within eye-sight of new Cadillacs as well as Bentleys, Lotus, Rolls Royces and Land Rovers (but, no salesman will interfere with your putting!) Daily competition is scored by the computer, and the winners are invited back at the end of each month for a friendly championship putt-off. The winner gets a round of golf at the world class Innesbrook Resort—a mere 5 miles north of the dealership.

(Note the "world-class" association between the dealership and the resort.)

Golf isn't your game? Or your needs are different on this particular day? Try the complimentary hand or neck massage on Tuesdays and Thursdays, Have the concierge book travel arrangements, make restaurant reservations for you, or locate tickets to an upcoming event.

There are oven-fresh cookies, coffee, popcorn newspapers, and even the suggestion of a lively round of bingo if enough customers are interested!

Rather than watching the 13" TV on the glass and chrome end table in a crowded service department lobby, you're treated to a 50-seat, surround-sound theatre with a 500 watt sound system and movies on schedule every two hours--all complimentary services of course.

There is no intercom system blaring throughout the dealership to remind you that you are simply a lost soul in a megastore, but sometime shortly before the movie starts, the concierge locates you in-person—wherever you may have wandered to-- and offers the next title while checking to ensure that your needs are being met.

If rugged adventure is more your style, you may choose to drive a new Land Rover on the enhanced Mountain and Jungle test tracks---all of this while your car is being serviced. By design, the hope is that these diversions have:

1) Made you feel more valued by the dealership and staff.

2) Provided you with entertainment options that will decrease your perceived waiting time.
3) Turned you, through this experience, into a loyal customer both for service and whenever you choose to purchase a new car in the future.
4) Delivered an experience you'll tell your colleagues, family and friends about, turning you into a viral marketer for the dealership.

If the objective is to *catch and release* so these customers will survive to be caught again, then the costs of creating this "*spookless*" experience must be weighed against the continuing value—indeed the life value— of the customer. From this perspective, the return on investment far outweighs the costs.

In your own business, I encourage you to reexamine the consumer or client experience. Start your redesign process by looking at the overall experience of doing business with your company from your customers' perspectives. Determine the weakest delivery points in their experience then carefully study and dissect those. Then start with a blank sheet of paper---*a fresh fly*—and design a new customer experience that works better for the *fish* and allows you to catch more of them every time. They will respond, and you will make more money!

7

Tackle with Laser Focus!

Are you equipped for success?

Earlier we talked about making the *fly* seem more interesting than the natural food supply to the fish in the stream.

Anglers spend countless hours learning to *read the stream*, discovering what the fish are feeding on and *matching the hatch*—choosing a fly that will differentiate their offer just enough to attract attention and catch the fish.

Ultimately however, it is the delivery of that fly that determines whether the fish find it interesting.

For a few moments before I share another example of excellent brand experience, let's take a look at our tackle---the equipment we use to position and present the fly to the fish.

To the fly angler, the rod is the tool for aim and distance in positioning the fly at the appropriate place in the stream. Length, weight and flexibility all play an important part. Let me suggest in our analogy that the fly rod represents the structure of your organization and similarly holds the keys to your ability to compete in your industry and the targeted market segment. It also represents your organization's flexibility in response to changing customer demands and preferences.

In the early going the fly reel does little more than house the line similar to your office or manufacturing or customer level facility.

But upon further examination, we discover four critical pieces of line between the core of the reel and the fly.

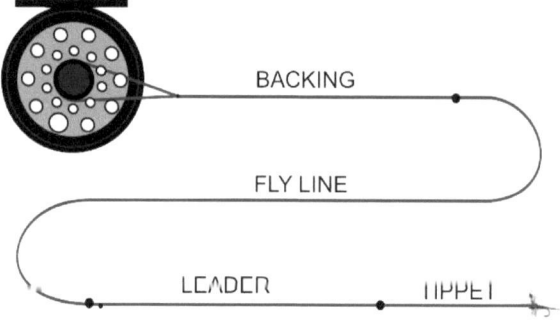

First loaded onto the reel is the fly line *backing* which exists between the core of the reel and the actual fly line. This piece of line operates much like the financial backing of your company, by ensuring additional resources are in place, should the *fish* respond wildly to the fly and exhaust the normal length of the fly line. It acts as a sort-of contingency plan so that just in case customers respond according to plan, you won't lose the *fish*, or an opportunity to continue *fishing* after this one is caught.

The actual fly line comes next in a variety of options depending on the experience of the angler and the fishing environment. In a business sense this represents the internal conduit that bridges the gap between what we offer and the target market that will most likely appreciate and value it.

At the end of the fly line we find the leader. Ironically this leader is closer to the fish than we find most management teams are to their customers. Yet to manage a unique, branded experience, the leader/visionary must have a pulse on the market and the direction the offer is taking to the customer.

While the fly line is typically an easily identifiable color, the leader is usually clear. True company leadership follows suite, not necessarily taking on the customer head-to-head, but close enough to keep the brand experience aligned with consumer preferences. No amount of activity at stream-level will differentiate you for success without a leader*ship* commitment.

The final piece of line is called the tippet, which connects the leader to the fly. This tiny piece of line—typically no more than 18 inches long is totally invisible to the fish. It represents the operational, logistical and financial workings required to finally place an attractive fly in front of a hungry fish.

The fish don't know and don't care what hoops the angler had to jump through to get to the stream, get dressed, assess the stream, match the hatch secure the fly and discover the location of the fish. Sound familiar?

It is.

Your customers simply don't care, and don't want to know what it takes to get your product or service to market. Just as with the fish, these logistics need to be out of sight in order to maintain focus on your offering, the experience and the benefits you deliver.

At last, the fly represents our offer to the fish. How accurate we are with the presentation, how we tweak the action of the fly, with feedback through the rod, our positioning and our accuracy in predicting the reaction of the fish –the total experience-- plays to our success. Timing, the right equipment and a laser focus is absolutely essential to delivering a valued customer experience.

8

Match The Hatch

Make the Experience Worth The Energy --
Build-a-Bear® --How to Turn an $18.00 teddy
bear into an $85.00 smile!

If you've ever been a parent or a grand-parent, you
understand the magic of a child's teddy bear.
Whether it is new or all but worn out it still
possesses a certain inalienable value to a child.
Because in most cases, a teddy bear is not just a
teddy bear. The reason the bear has value to the
child is connected to an experience, a location, a
destination, who gave it to them, how cuddly the
bear feels, what color the bear may be or the
clothing that makes THIS bear so special.

Enter a group called "Build-A-Bear®", now
headquartered in St. Louis, MO. This
entrepreneurial group took a simple concept—
owning a favorite teddy bear—and rediscovered
all of the reasons why a teddy bear is important to
the child—just as we did simply in the previous
paragraph.

The magic of their concept however was to put each child in charge of creating the reasons why a teddy from Build-a Bear would be their most cherished Teddy bear!

They actually challenged themselves to "think like the fish'—like the customer—the child in this case.

The questions were:

1. "What if the child could be involved in every step of the creation (to a reasonable level)?
2. What if each step in the experience of building your own teddy bear could offer choices that would result in a unique, one-of-a kind bear?
3. Would this experience make the bear and the child inseparable?
4. Would it make the value of the bear worth a premium?
5. Could the premium carry a profitable price-tag?
6. Could one experience result in multiple experiences or an extended life-value of the customer?

The answers were not quite as easy as the questions, although some assumptions were easy to make. Here's what Build-a-Bear did to succeed:

After settling on a mall location, with likely "push-past" exposure to mom and the kids, they created a teddy bear factory of sorts. The environment is designed for immediate kid-acceptance from the colors to the graphics, to the merchandising of the intended experience. *They have carefully chosen the right fly to match the hatch.*

Following some preliminary briefing by the kid/parent friendly staff, each child begins the process of building the bear by picking out what he/she perceives to be the perfect bear, based upon color, nap of the fur, etc. (The child does is actually pick out the pre-sewn body shell of the bear.)

At subsequent stations along the way, the child determines how fluffy or firm the bear should be, and what color and size the eyes and other features should be. It becomes a total immersion experience in consumerism, yet designed to maintain a high level of safety for the child and appropriate involvement of the parent who will after all be paying the bill before the child re-enters the mainstream of traffic in the mall.

Ultimately the experience and the reaction of the child will eclipse the bill. Likely the experience will never be forgotten. The bill will be lost to the memories. The memories will be shared with those who have yet to experience it. The customers will build the brand.

9

The Perfect Catch

....and I thought it was just the closest dry cleaner!

If you've ever moved cross county, you've been through the experience of setting up some basic relationships: a bank, a family doctor, a church, and car servicing and oh yes, the laundry.

Such was the case when I moved to the front range of the Rocky Mountains.

A laundry at first is simply a place to drop off the shirts and suits. The closest one to my new home was about 2 blocks away. Summit Cleaners looked a bit like a branch bank, complete with a drive thru.

On my first stop, I parked and took what was by then a mountain of laundry into the front counter where I was greeted then asked the big question, "Do you have an account with us?"

Typically when the question catches me off guard, I have a tendency to respond in kind. "Why, do I need one?" I fired back.

Kindly they let me know that it wasn't necessary, but that if I did, they would be able to keep my cleaning preferences on file in their computers,

would provide me with personalized laundry bags, and keep the credit or debit card number that I preferred to use on file—making the entire process of drop off and pick-up take less than 60 seconds!

Oh, and if I came to pick-up my laundry after hours---anytime, I could pick it up through their convenient store-side kiosk!

With one question, they had opened the opportunity to *deliver the fly* and make the offer *better than the natural.*

I was hooked!

Most of the time, things ran smoothly, just like they had predicted.

Occasionally when I dropped by after hours, I slid my card through a slot on the side of the kiosk and magic began to happen: The inner door of the kiosk opened and a pipe slid down at an angle from inside the store to the front door of the kiosk. The carousel began to move and automatically my clothing was picked- my shirts, my pants, and my suits all began to slide down the pipe hanging them all right before me.

When finished, the inside door would close, and the outside door would open. All I had to do was lift my clothing out and carry them to my car. What an experience!

Late one night as I packed for an out-of-town business trip, I realized I had forgotten to pick up the suit I intended to wear. I zipped around the corner to the cleaners, but for the first time, the kiosk didn't work.

The number on the front of the kiosk put me straight through to the owner, who promised that if I would stay put, he would be there within nine minutes to solve the problem. I did. And he did. Amazing!

In our metaphor, the original *fly* had not worked, but he had adjusted his "fly"- *matched the hatch*, and delivered something more enticing, keeping my interest.

I was not only hooked, but I was loyal and my reviews were five star! After more than 2 years of doing business with Summit Cleaners, I must admit, I finally looked at the first bill attached to the clothing.

The brand experience had eclipsed the cost of the services. The convenience was worth the premium. Summit Cleaners was MY cleaners.

No other provider stood a chance of penetrating that loyalty.

10

The Perfect Brand Experience

How you can make yours the experience worth
loyalty (and in the process a premium price)?

This small book has included many examples of
successful experiential branding.

In every case these companies *matched the hatch*
by discovering how to inject differences in the
experience of doing business with them that really
made a difference to their ideal market.

They *chose the fly* that made the offer better than
the *natural alternatives*—their competition.

It takes thought, research, conversations with
customers and a study of the customers'
behavior—what makes them come, stay, and
leave, and say great things –leave reviews that
drive your future business. It takes an analysis of
the entire interchange between company and
customer and an inventiveness that can morph the
mundane into a priceless experience.

To Discover More about The Power of
Online Reputation Marketing, visit:

OnlineReputationTrust.com

For corporate and organizational meetings or
executive fly fishing retreats on this and other
branding issues including:
- Online Reputation Marketing
- Online Display Advertising
- Mobile Marketing

Contact:
info@advancedsmallbusinessmarketing.com

---

*Now, just for fun, visit your nearest fly
fishing shop – just to see how this works
on the leisure side of the stream!*

www.ingramcontent.com/pod-product-compliance
Lightning Source LLC
Chambersburg PA
CBHW040841180526
45159CB00001B/264